C000135266

Picturesque
CORNWALL

Described by Reginald J. W. Hammond
with Foreword by S. P. B. Mais

Painted by George F. Nicholls, L. Mortimer
and H. Sylvester Stannard R.A.

SALMON

Published by
J Salmon Limited
100 London Road, Sevenoaks,
Kent TN13 1BB

First edition 1995

Designed by the Salmon Studio

Copyright © 1995 J Salmon Limited

ISBN 1 898435 42 1

All rights reserved. No part of this publi-
cation may be reproduced, stored in a
retrieval system, or transmitted, in any
form or by any means, electronic,
mechanical, photocopying, recording or
otherwise, nor may any of the illustrations be framed, mounted or converted in
any manner for resale, without the prior
permission of the copyright holder.

Neither this book nor any part or any of
the illustrations, photographs or repro-
ductions contained in it shall be sold or
disposed of otherwise than as a complete
book and any unauthorised sale of such
part illustration photograph or reproduc-
tion shall be deemed to be a breach of the
Publisher's Copyright.

Printed in England by
J Salmon Limited, Tubs Hill Works
Sevenoaks, Kent

AN OLD CORNER, ST. IVES

Coloured Illustrations

"THE MAGIC OF CORNWALL"

Lanyon Quoit

ALTHOUGH NO SIGNS on the Devon border proclaim Cornwall as a separate land, it nevertheless remains apart from the rest of England, and a Cornishman has to "cross the border" as much as any Scot, when entering England. From Launceston to Land's End the country stretches out, a windswept backbone of granite and grey stone, where the mystery of Jamaica Inn still lingers and Bodmin Moor greets one with sweeping views in summer and with drifting mists in winter.

But leave the moors, and their wandering cattle, to wind one's way down the valleys, past squat grey farms or old mineworkings and clay-pits; in the South, to follow some picturesque river and find an old fishing port or sheltered cove, perhaps now partially a modern resort, possibly still as it was a hundred years ago; in the North, suddenly to see a magnificent view of the Atlantic and then to descend a twisting road to an unseen coastal village. From these places arise the legends of smugglers and Cornish "piskies". In these places remain the names of saints unknown in any other part of England, and here Cornish pasties and saffron cakes are more popular than any delicacies of English cooking.

Let us then take a look at some of these places and see how the unique character and beauty of the Cornish coast attracts visitors from every part of the land, and makes Cornishmen proud of their "Celtic Corner" of England.

OLD COTTAGES AT POLPERRO

The Castle and Harbour, Fowey

FROM LOOE TO MEVAGISSEY

LOOE, IN THE SOUTH-EAST corner of Cornwall, has a double role as one of the chief fishing ports of the county and as a popular holiday resort. East and West sections of the town sit either side of the narrow Looe River at a particularly lovely stretch of the coast. Ferries crossing the harbour mouth are useful, for the road bridge, a graceful seven-arch structure, lies half a mile upstream. Small fishing boats provide colour and interest to the harbour scene. There is a sandy beach, good sea and river fishing and boating, and plenty of sport.

East Looe's quaint, narrow and crooked streets and several curious old buildings delight the eye. The Old Guildhall, now a museum, with the old stocks and one of the last pillories still in existence, dates from the seventeenth-century. The stone "Banjo" pier is a popular promenade. At West Looe's quayside is the little Church of St Nicholas, with low tower and campanile. Modern buildings line the top of the cliff road to Hannafore overlooking a bathing beach to the little Looe, or St George's Island a half mile out to sea.

The main road for Talland cuts across wooded hillsides, but a cliff-top path can be followed round to Talland Church, rich in carved bench-ends, and having a separate tower, then on to Talland Sand, a pleasant bathing beach in a beautiful setting.

Polperro is a pretty little fishing village of cement-washed and grey stone cottages huddled round a tiny harbour where the little

West Looe

River Pol and a road descend steeply through a narrow cleft in wild rocky cliffs. Picturesque cottages rise one behind the other from the water's edge, up the steeply sloping hillside. Curious old buildings abut each other in narrow courts and alleyways. Of interest is the Smuggling Museum in the former home of Dr Jonathan Couch, grandfather of Sir Arthur Quiller Couch, the famous Cornish writer. Near the Roman Bridge is the curious House-on-the-Props.

LOOE FROM THE DOWNS

POLPERRO HARBOUR

BODINNICK-BY-FOWEY

FOWEY HARBOUR

The harbour is always busy with its fishing boats. Mackerel, crab and lobster are the principal catches and small shark are frequently brought in. West of the breakwater is Chapel Cliff, a truly fine viewpoint. Below the cliff is a swimming pool set in the rocks.

Fowey, larger than Polperro but still quaint, with narrow streets and colourful houses, lies on the estuary of the River Fowey. It is a

The Harbour, Polperro

good centre for sailing and sea-fishing, and bathing is possible from the sandy Readymoney Cove and several nearby rocky inlets. A car-ferry crosses the river to Bodinnick with its old cottages and Ferry Inn and breakneck hill. Nearer the mouth a motor boat service runs to Polruan, from which fine cliff walks may be enjoyed.

The Fowey is navigable for small boats for six miles to Lostwithiel, a picturesque old town with a medieval bridge, thirteenth-century

Duchy Palace and interesting Guildhall. A mile to the north is Restormel Castle, a great stone keep standing on a huge circular motte or mound known to have been built up in the year 1100. The pretty Luxulyan Valley attracts many visitors. Another popular excursion is to Lanhydrock House, set in a great park and famous for its picture gallery and fine plaster ceilings.

Bodinnick from Fowey

Westward of Fowey is the placid St Austell Bay. St Austell, with its lovely little heritage harbour of Charlestown and modern port of Par, is the centre of the china clay industry. The huge mounds of waste material are a feature of the landscape. In the wide bay Par, Carlyon, Duporth and Porth-pean all have sandy and safe bathing beaches.

Mevagissey is a picturesque old-world fishing village. The double harbour, busy with small fishing boats and pleasure craft, is the major attraction here but there is pleasant bathing from the nearby sand and shingle Polstreath beach. South westward beyond the bold headland of Dodman Point, Veryan Bay and Gerrans Bay curve either side of Nare Head from which, and also from nearby Carne Beacon, there are some wonderful coastal views.

THE OLD BRIDGE, LOSTWITHIEL

ST. AUSTELL BAY FROM PENARE ROCKS

THE INNER HARBOUR, MEVAGISSEY

FLUSHING FROM FALMOUTH

Falmouth Harbour

FALMOUTH AND ROSELAND

THE HEYDAY OF FALMOUTH, lying on one of England's finest natural harbours, was in connection with the Mail Packet service, which flourished here from 1688 to 1850. The romance and excitement of that period will bear comparison with those of the old sea-adventurers when maritime doings were mainly piratical. On the eastern side of the great estuary is the Roseland district, crowded with spots as lovely as its name; a name which bears no reference to roses but is borrowed from the old Cornish word *ros* meaning moorland or heath.

St Mawes, well situated on a wooded inlet, is a favourite spot for yachting people and artists, and a good centre for excursions in the beautiful Roseland peninsula; to Portscatho clustered around its tiny harbour, to little Portloe with boats drawn up on the slipway, to the curious round cottages at Veryan and to the ancient church of St Just-in-Roseland nestling into the hillside beside the creek. The castle is one of the chain of defences set up by Henry VIII in

1540, and overlooks Carrick Roads across which is a ferry service to Falmouth, a popular holiday resort, seaport and yachting centre with busy harbour, sandy beaches and fine gardens. There are good sports facilities, a golf course and various entertainments. The estuary of the River Fal has innumerable beautiful little creeks

King Harry Ferry

which can be explored by boat, and a trip to Truro, with its fine cathedral is a popular excursion. Smaller, but equally beautiful, is the wooded inlet of the Helford River, immortalised by Daphne Du Maurier in her novel *Frenchman's Creek*. On the summit of Pendennis Point is Pendennis Castle, contemporary with the castle at St Mawes across the estuary.

TRURO CATHEDRAL

THE COAST NEAR THE LIZARD

The Lizard Point

THE LIZARD

IN THESE DAYS of rapid and easy travel, many come to the Lizard from Penzance and St. Ives, from Falmouth and even from as far as Newquay, for a single day's enjoyment; and are usually content if they have seen Kynance Cove and the famous lighthouse.

But these are not the whole of the Lizard. There is here, in this peninsula from Helford to Loe Pool, the wildest scenery of rocks, cliffs and the sea, and the softest, most luxuriant scenery of an inland valley. Among these valleys and tiny fishing havens, and on the wooded tops of the hills, there are flowers around every cottage and hedgerows filled with fuchsias and honeysuckle. The coast is broken and varied with dark or warmly-coloured rocks, white sands, hovering gulls and the deep blue and green and purple waters crashing, thunderously at times, among the crags, caves and chasms.

Across Goonhilly Down, with its surrealistic telecommunication dishes probing the skies, the road leads direct across the Lizard Peninsula to Lizard Point, the southernmost extremity of mainland England. To east and west splendid cliff walks may be enjoyed in some of the finest coast scenery of Britain. The lighthouse is a popular attraction. The local serpentine rock, coloured and mottled, is fashioned into attractive ornaments and souvenirs. Houzel Bay,

Mullion Cove

immediately east of Lizard Point, has a popular sandy beach. Close by are many delightful little coves such as Cadgwith, Coverack, Porthoustock and Porthallow to delight the visitor. The west coast of the Lizard Peninsula is far-famed with such delectable spots as Kynance Cove, Mullion Cove and Poldhu before it tails away into Mount's Bay and the little harbour of Porthleven. Nearby is Helston, a busy market town and the scene each May of the well-known Flora or Furry Dance.

KYNANCE COVE

ST. MICHAEL'S MOUNT

St. Michael's Mount

MOUNT'S BAY

There is nothing quite like St. Michael's Mount on the English coast; for its parallel one must go to the Mont St. Michel of Normandy. In certain respects there is a resemblance to Holy Island, the ancient Lindisfarne off the Northumbrian shore; but St. Michael's Mount has its own distinction and an even greater wealth of association. The accuracy of its old Cornish name, the "hoar rock in the wood", has been proved by geologists and to this day it is only insular at high tide, although it is some two thousand years since this part of Mount's Bay was a marshy woodland. A religious foundation existed here in the time of Edward the Confessor and later the place became a secular as well as a religious stronghold.

St Michael's Mount stands out to sea opposite Marazion in beautiful Mount's Bay. It may be reached by boat or on foot by a stone causeway at low tide. On the summit of the rock is the picturesque castle and fourteenth-century chapel. At the head of Mount's Bay is

PENZANCE HARBOUR

OLD NEWLYN

Penzance, a popular resort with sand and shingle beach and fine gardens where palms and sub-tropical plants flourish. The harbour is the mainland terminus for the Isles of Scilly steamer ferry service. Just a mile away lies the picturesque fishing village of Newlyn. It

Mousehole

has a good modern harbour, one of the country's foremost fishing ports, and a fine sandy beach for bathing. Nearby is the quaint fishing village of Mousehole with twisting streets and alleys and a little harbour cluttered with brightly coloured boats.

There is a fine cliff walk over to Lamorna Cove, picturesque and rocky where an old stone quay stands at the foot of a steep wooded combe. At Porthcurno Bay, one of the finest of the Cornish coves, golden shell sand, magnificent granite cliffs, and a vari-coloured sea make an unforgettable picture; the little open-air Minack Theatre on the cliff top is of interest for the plays performed here during the summer.

LAMORNA COVE

LAND'S END

Enys Dodman and the Armed Knight

LANDS END TO ST. IVES

THIS IS A LAND that, for unknown centuries, has had to confront the utmost fierceness of Atlantic seas and Atlantic winds. The waters have carved its contour and have shaped it into an appearance of embattled bulwarks and castellated crags with the finest coast scenery lying northwards between St. Just and St. Ives. Legend says that miles upon miles of land have been torn away by these devastating seas, so that the true Land's End must once have been at Scilly or beyond. Be that as it may, Land's End is the western-most point of England with 60-foot high granite cliffs. On calm days the spot serves as a good viewpoint for the lone Wolf Rock, the

Longships Lighthouse, or the distant Isles of Scilly. But when a south west gale rages the place is transformed into a roaring fury of pounding waves and shattered spray. To the north lies the wide Whitesand Bay with Sennen Cove tucked below the cliffs. The sandy beach here is ideal for surfing. St Just, a one-time tin mining centre, has an interesting old church notable for its wall paintings.

Cape Cornwall juts out to sea to form the southern headland of

Gurnard's Head

Porthledden Bay whilst northwards, beyond the old Botallack and Levant tin mines, is Pendeen where the lighthouse may be visited. In the farmhouse of Pendeen, Dr Borlase the well-known Cornish historian and antiquary was born in 1695. Close to the farm is a Cornish "fougou", or hiding place.

Beyond Porthmeor is some of the grandest and wildest cliff scenery of Cornwall. The rugged promontories of Gurnard's Head and Zennor Head jut seawards with many little rock-bound sandy

ST. IVES FROM PORTHMINSTER

CARBIS BAY, ST. IVES

coves between. At Zennor is a logan or rocking stone, and one of the largest cromlechs or prehistoric burial places in England.

Set in a beautiful bay of golden sands and with a fascinating harbour, the colourful fishing port of St Ives is a popular resort and a favourite haunt of artists. Old houses and quaint narrow alleys cluster round the harbour against a narrow neck of land either side

The Logan Rock

of which are magnificent sands: Porthminster Beach calm and safe, Porthmeor open to the Atlantic breakers and famed for surfing. To the east are Carbis Bay, another fine sandy beach, and the popular golf links on the sandhills of Lelant overlooking the sea. The village of Lelant with an ancient church is on the River Hayle where some good fishing is to be had in the estuary. Splendid views of the coast and surrounding country may be obtained from Trencrom Hill a few miles to the south west.

THE ARCHED AND CHAPEL ROCKS, PERRANPORTH

Trevaunance Cove, St. Agnes

ST. IVES TO NEWQUAY

Cornwall is a happy hunting-ground for holidaymakers and Newquay is the queen of Cornish watering places; but away from the beaten track there are sanctuaries of solitude to be discovered.

Portreath lies at the foot of the lovely wooded Portreath Valley up which a road runs to Redruth. Cliffside houses look down on a narrow harbour and sandy beach. Out to sea stands Gull Rock. St Agnes, a one-time tin mining centre, is built on the slopes of a wooded valley which leads down to the delightful Trevaunance Cove where boating and bathing are first-class and where many little warm rock pools, abounding with tiny marine creatures and colourful sea-anemones, are left by the receding tide. St Agnes Head on the coast and St Agnes Beacon a little inland are two fine viewpoints here.

Perranporth is a popular resort backed by extensive sand dunes. It has a magnificent firm sandy beach and sports facilities including tennis and golf. A favourite excursion is to St Piran's Church, a sixth-century foundation rescued from the drifting sand, and St Piran's Round, an ancient amphitheatre where the old Cornish miracle plays were once performed. The village of Crantock is a delightful place, its bay and headlands are fine and the Gannel itself a lovely river at full tide.

Crantock Church

Newquay is the principal holiday resort of North Cornwall with a considerable accommodation capacity for visitors. The town stands on high cliffs towering above a small harbour and magnificent tide-washed sands which extend through a series of interlinked bays for several miles. Surfing is first-rate and there are numerous sports and entertainment facilities. The harbour was at one time busy with pilchard fishing and the Huer's House on Towan Head, from which the look-out or "huer" gave warning of the approach of a shoal, is an interesting survival of those times. West of the town lies magnificent Fistral Bay where surfing (with care) is unsurpassed. A little inland is Trerice Manor, a fine sixteenth-century manor house which is notable for its plaster ceilings.

NEWQUAY HARBOUR

PADSTOW HARBOUR

The Saddle Rock, Bude

THE NORTH-EAST COAST

THIS IS A COAST both wide and grand, noble if at times desolate, with coves and caverns and surf-dashed rocks.

Watergate Bay stretches northward for four miles of very fine cliff scenery with many indentations where sandy porths or coves provide wonderful bathing. Watergate itself stands at the foot of a steep cleft in the hills. Mawgan Porth where the wooded Vale of Lanherne opens to the sea has an ideal surfing beach, but at Bedruthan Steps, a famed beauty spot, one must be content to view the shore from the cliff top.

Padstow is an ancient port on the Camel estuary popular now as a centre for boating and sailing. On May Day each year the quaint Hobby Horse Dance takes place in the streets. St Petroc's Church is of interest and has some fine stained glass. Good bathing beaches near at hand include Harbour Cove and the sandy Harlyn Bay. The lighthouse on Trevose Head is a fine viewpoint and the life-boat house is worth a visit.

Rock stands opposite Padstow on the Camel with a ferry connection.

It is a grand spot for sailing and there is golf at nearby St Enodoc. The old church by the links was once buried by drifting sand. From Polzeath, yet another splendid surfing beach, there is a bracing clifftop walk to Pentire Point.

Boscastle is a pretty little village at the foot of a steep wooded valley through which the Valency river tumbles to the sea. A fascinating little harbour is almost land-locked by great rugged cliffs. The beach is rocky and a fine blowhole adds excitement in rough

Padstow Harbour

weather. Tintagel, famous for its legends of King Arthur, lies at a wild and impressive stretch of the coast. The ruins of the Norman castle stand on a great rugged promontory 270 feet above the sea. Of interest in the village are the fourteenth-century Old Post Office and the stone-built King Arthur's Hall.

Southward of Tintagel are the fine sands of Trebarwith Strand whilst inland is the ancient town of Camelford, Tennyson's "Camelot", and a good centre for excursions to Rough Tor and Brown Willy the two highest points of Bodmin Moor and to Jamaica Inn. Further south is quaint Port Isaac where a boat may be hired for mackerel fishing or a bathe taken in tiny Porthquin Bay.

THE CASTLE, TINTAGEL

THE HARBOUR ENTRANCE, BOSCASTLE

The popular resort of Bude stands in an open situation in a break in the high Cornish cliffs. The turf-covered common of Summerleaze Down separates the town from the sea. Here there are facilities for various sports and some entertainment, but the chief activity is the marvellous surfing, as great Atlantic breakers come tumbling in to magnificent sandy beaches. Popular excursions can be made to Poughill with an old church famous for its coloured frescoes, to the thickly wooded Combe Valley, to Penfound Manor, one of the oldest inhabited manors in England and finally to

Morwenstow

Morwenstow. Here Parson Hawker lived and laboured, writing his poems and growing famous by his eccentricities. He is best remembered for his "Song of the Western Men" with the lines

> "And shall Trelawney die?
> Here's twenty thousand Cornishmen
> Will know the reason why!"

As we leave Bude we also leave Cornwall, a county that man can only change in parts; ruled by Nature but unconquered by the seas and winds that beat relentlessly against its granite cliffs and sandy shores.

COMPASS POINT, BUDE